GARY LIBRARY
VERMONT COLLEGE

W9-BWH-181

WITHDRAWN

NEW FOOTPRINTS
OF THE TROJAN HORSE

American Viewpoint Series
   Textbooks for Junior High Schools
We and Our Work—*Johnson*
We and Our History—*Hart*
We and Our Government—*Jenks*
We and Our Constitution—*Hart*
The Spirit of America—*Patri*

American Viewpoint Little Books
Know Your Isms—*Dodge*

NEW FOOTPRINTS

OF THE

TROJAN

THE COMMUNIST PROGRAM

Published for American Viewpoint by
FARRAR, STRAUS & YOUNG, INC.
New York

HORSE

TO CONQUER THE WORLD

HERBERT CARLETON MAYER
President, American Viewpoint, Inc.

ILLUSTRATED BY JACK BETTS
Introduction by General Lucius D. Clay

1952

Library of Congress Catalog Number 52-6975

Copyright 1952 by American Viewpoint, Inc.
All rights reserved including the right to
reproduce this book, or portions thereof in any form.
Manufactured in the United States of America
by H. Wolff, New York

947.085
M468n

To Jane, Bert and Ann
Whose Generation Must Again Prove
The American Idea

105 15

CONTENTS

CONTENTS

Today, the free world fights for survival. Physically, it fights in Korea, Indo-China, and Malaya. Economically, it is fighting on all fronts. Concurrently, the free world is progressing in its efforts to increase its physical and economic strengths. There is reason to hope for an early balancing of power which will ease the threat of Communist aggression and, perhaps, bring about an armed truce, if not true peace.

However, the struggle to capture the minds of men will continue unabated. The lie, continually repeated and unchallenged, tends to obscure the truth. The extravagant promises of Communism sound attractive until they are exposed as lies.

If the free world is to win in this ideological struggle, its people must understand the real meaning of Communism. This requires access to simply explained basic facts.

Herbert Carleton Mayer has undertaken this task in "Trojan Horse." While with military government in Germany, he became familiar with Communist tactics and participated in the use of truth in counterattack. The knowledge gained from practical experience as well as long study is expressed in an unusual but highly effective manner in "Trojan Horse." I know of no simpler way to a basic understanding of Communism than by reading it. I hope it will be read by many thousands.

LUCIUS D. CLAY
General, Retired
U. S. Army

This little book has really been written by the hundreds of people who asked for help in understanding the "cold war"—students, businessmen, teachers, housewives—worried about the growth of collectivist ideas.

The original book, *Footprints of the Trojan Horse*, printed in 1940, told the story of the Nazi and Fascist propaganda war. The proof of its need was the distribution of more than three and a half million copies. Growing demand in recent months for similar help compelled the writing of this *New Footprints of the Trojan Horse*.

There is no doubt of the intentions of the Kremlin toward the world and toward the United States. But if the Politburo's Communist ideas are dangerous to us, so are our American ideas even more dangerous to Communism. The way to fight an idea is with a better idea, The American Idea.

HERBERT CARLETON MAYER

THE LEGEND OF THE
TROJAN HORSE

For ten long years the city of Troy
Withstood the assaults of the Greek army.

Finally the Greeks withdrew as if to go home,
Built a huge wooden horse
Concealing Greek spies within its body,
And dragged it to the city walls by night.
Morning revealed the strange creature.
Perhaps it was a gift of the gods
Commemorating the departure of the Greeks,
Why not take it into the city?
Reasoned the Trojans.
So in went the wooden horse,
Into the city that could not be conquered

From without.

That night the hidden Greeks came out
Stole up on the guards and slew them
And opened the city gates
To the returned Greek army.
So Troy fell, for all its brave men,
Not because its people did not fight valiantly
But just because they failed to protect themselves

From the enemy within.

That harmless looking Trojan Horse!

Since 1814
Kings, emperors, and dictators
Have threatened America with invasion
But they never set foot on western soil.

Two great oceans
And friendly, peaceful neighbors
Made this world safe.
  Now a new tyrant
Plans to take America,
Not by military conquest,
But by capture from within,
By infiltration—

the Red Trojan Horse.

NEW FOOTPRINTS
OF THE TROJAN HORSE

I

THREE PLANNED IT

Communism,
Like all great movements,
Has its great names,
The men who started the idea,
And those who added to it
As it grew and developed.

Three great Communists,
And only three,
Are universally honored:

KARL MARX

NICOLAI LENIN

JOSEPH STALIN

KARL MARX—the Originator

Son of the German ghetto,
Bitter against life as he saw it,
Marx dreamed of a workers' revolution
To destroy all in authority.

Driven out of Germany for his beliefs,
He fled to Holland, and then to England,
Where he lived out his life on charity.
Marx proclaimed that:
Only workers produce wealth;
all others are parasites;
Therefore workers must rebel
and claim their rights,
Setting up a dictatorship of the workers,
Exterminating the middle class,
Wiping out the leaders,
Replacing all government,
Controlling all life.
This is the "bible" of the Communist!

4

NICOLAI LENIN—the Organizer

Marx's great disciple was LENIN.

He traveled widely building up the party,

Planning for the day of revolution.

Finally he saw his chance in Russia,

Seized control of Kerensky's elected government.

Under his leadership, Red troops—

    Imprisoned the Douma (Parliament),

      Drove out or murdered officials,

        Slaughtered the nobility,

          Let loose a reign of terror.

As head of the Union of Soviet Socialist Republics

LENIN accomplished three things:

    Organized Russia as the first Communist nation;

    Defended Russia against non-Communist enemies;

      Made Russia the center of the new Communist
        International.

At his death in 1924

His tomb in the Red Square

Became the shrine for Communists

Throughout the world.

5

JOSEPH STALIN—the Dictator

Born Joseph Vissarionovich Dzugashvili
In Georgia (Russia), trained for the priesthood,
He renounced his vows, turned revolutionary.
Gaining a reputation for violence
Through robbery, murder, and sabotage,
Lenin nicknamed him Stalin, steel,
So he became Joseph Stalin.

As secretary of the Communist party
He took control when Lenin died,
Outlawed Trotsky and the old Bolsheviks,
Sent millions to their death or Siberia
Until he was supreme dictator
Without rival or threat.

STALIN made Russia into a world power
By driving Russia ruthlessly to progress,
By defending Russia against Hitler's attack,
By extending Soviet influence over satellite lands,
By expanding the Red program to control the world.

2

THE MARCH OF
RED CONQUEST

Today STALIN rules Russia
And the new Soviet Empire
Of Communists throughout the world.

This march of Red Empire took:
Eastern Poland in the deal with Hitler,
Parts of Finland as the spoils of war,
Latvia, Lithuania, Esthonia
And East Germany by conquests;
Bessarabia from Rumania,
The Kuriles and half of Sakhalin from Japan.
All these were swallowed up
By the Kremlin's new juggernaut,

Spoils of conquest.

But Red conquest does not stop there.
Free nations became satellites
And satellites became puppet lands

9

All governed from the Kremlin.

    Rumania

    Bulgaria

    Hungary

    Albania

    Poland

      Czechoslovakia

Each in the grip of the Red tyrant

With captive governments directed from Moscow

To rule farms

    industries

    business

    homes

      schools

        churches

        and all cultural life

As Stalin dictates.

THE RED TROJAN HORSE.

In 1948, the REDS took Czechoslovakia

Not by military force

              but by infiltration.

While Russia's relations with the Czechs
Were being hailed by leftists the world over
As proof of Stalin's neighborly attitude
The Czech Communist Party was quietly at work
Putting members in key positions
In government, industry, commerce, and cultural affairs,
And setting up secret ACTION COMMITTEES.
By 1948 the Red Trojan Horse
Was in the market place
With its hidden spies ready
To open the gates to the waiting Communists.

The freedom-loving Czechs
Forgot the lesson of the Trojan Horse
And fell victim
            to the enemy within.

PATTERN FOR CONQUEST

   The fall of Czechoslovakia
Awoke the careless people of the world
To the threat of COMMUNIST world domination.

At last the leaders saw the danger
Not just in the huge Red Military force,
But in the organized Red underground,—
The Cominform designed to promote
World revolution and destruction
By secret undermining of the nation's strength
Like termites eating out the timbers of the house,
Until the structure falls of its own weight.

The strategy of world revolution,
Of Soviet domination of the earth
Is just the old device
                    of infiltration.
The Red Trojan Horse.

3

TRAIL OF THE TROJAN HORSE

IN GREECE—

World War II ended in Europe on May 8, 1945,
But not for the Greeks
Hitler's bloody Nazis were gone,
But the Red Partisans were there
Desperately fighting to take Greece—

for STALIN

Public buildings were destroyed,
Factories and warehouses were raided,
Loyal leaders were murdered,
Children were kidnapped,
Whole villages were slaughtered.
The Greek army could not defeat the Reds
Armed and fed by Communist satellites.
Not until the United States
Sent military equipment and supplies,
And a special military mission

15

Did loyal Greeks finally save their nation.
Now Greece holds the uneasy line

against the Kremlin!

IN GERMANY—

Hitler, Goering, and Goebbels are dead;
But the rebuilding of Germany
As a peace-loving friendly nation lags
For STALIN will not keep his promises.
The Allied Control Council
Set up to govern Germany as a unit is gone.
Instead of one Germany, learning ways of peace,
There is West Germany,

East Germany,

and Berlin.

WEST GERMANY—

Guided and protected by the western nations,
Rebuilding, working, winning self-respect.

E.C.A. funds, technical aid,
And help of foreign purchasers
Are putting German industry on its feet again.
Cultural exchange programs have brought
The leaders of West Germany
Back in touch with the life of the world.
West Germany is building solidly
For the future in the best traditions
Of Old Germany's industry
science
culture.

EAST GERMANY—

Occupied by the predatory Red Army
Robbing, beating, raping helpless Germans,
Stripping industries, power plants, railroads,
And even taking old automobiles, furniture, clothing.
The people exploited and regimented
By the Politburo's propaganda machine.
Its schools strait-jacketed,
Its churches hamstrung by bureaucrats,

Its industry nationalized,
Its culture Stalinized,–
Helpless victim of Red tyranny.

BERLIN—

  Symbol of the unhappy divided nation,
Part slave and part becoming free,
Harassed, worried, fearful of Red might,
Behind the "Iron Curtain."
Yet Berlin stands stubbornly against the Soviets
Defying the RED hoodlums'
Rioting and kidnapping;
Lifting itself in living rebellion
Against the boasts and threats
Of STALIN'S henchmen
Against the little isle of freedom,

                                        Surrounded Berlin.

  Germany, divided by the RED imperialism,
Germany, half free, and gaining strength
To free the half that groans

Under the oppression the Reds call "peace."
Germany is trampled by the RED FOOTPRINTS
Of the Soviet's Trojan Horse.

IN ITALY—

Twice since the fighting stopped in Italy
Has this nation, struggling for rebirth,
Battled for its life in general elections
Against the Italian COMMUNIST Party
Led by Moscow-trained Togliatti
And his Red lieutenants
Directed by the Kremlin's plan of action,
Financed by the Red Cominform funds.
   The program of division
                                 confusion
                                      sabotage
Keeps Italy weak
Its government struggling
To bring order out of chaos—

                                 Imported from Red Russia
By the RED Trojan Horse.

IN FRANCE—

A powerful Communist Party
Controlling almost 40% of the popular vote
With its Trojan Horse tactics
Keeps a strangle hold on labor unions,
Paralyzes government service
With its grip on civil servants,
Holds its sway over scientists,
And even honeycombs the French Army.
  By fomenting crippling strikes,
By compounding continual confusion
In government
The REDS keep France crippled and weak.
Always in danger
From the RED enemy within.

IN CHINA—

The "agrarian reformers freeing the masses"

Have turned out to be dyed-in-the wool
Kremlin operatives.
   The familiar formula of protecting
The worker from the owner,
The tenant from the landlord,
Has become the usual land allotment,

                              crop quotas
                                 national levies
                                    confiscation,
Enforced by secret police
                    concentration camps
                         and death.
Today Mao Tse-tung, the tool of the POLITBURO
Holds China prostrate to the will of the KREMLIN
Raking STALIN'S chestnuts out of the Korean fire.
The old story of the Reds seizing a nation
By Trojan Horse tactics.

IN SOUTHEAST ASIA—

   And what of southeast Asia?
With its RED-incited rebels in Indonesia,

Or its open civil war in Indo-China
Led by RED-trained revolutionaries;
Or the Philippines with its RED Hukbalahaps
Spreading murder and rapine
Against a government trying to rebuild
After four years of occupation.

Or Korea divided by RED stubbornness,
Swept by the holocaust of civil war,
Korea, now the symbol
Of united effort against aggression,
Korea, after years of servitude and exploitation,
Bloody, but dreaming for freedom and peace.

IN ENGLAND—

Nor have the footprints of the Trojan Horse
Passed Britain, Mother of Parliaments,
Cradle of the Anglo-Saxon dream of liberty;
England the rugged mistress of the seas,
Who dared to stand alone
Against the worst Hitler's Luftwaffe could give,

And beat him back until help came.

England, strangled by recurring strikes

Planned and directed by RED agents,

Shaken by the Fuchs scandal of high treason

Of delivering atomic secrets to the REDS;

England whose Fabian Socialists

Thought they could play with fire

And not get burned.

Today England hardly knows her strength

Or weakness, not being able to gauge

The inroads of the Red Trojan Horse.

IN THE AMERICAS—

From Alaska to Chile lead

The RED footprints of the Trojan Horse,

Marked by riots and strikes,

Spying and treachery.

The bloody riots at the Pan American Conference

Showed the RED strength.

RED rebellion and dictatorship

In Central American nations,
RED riots in Puerto Rico and Cuba.
Canada's spy ring
To steal atomic secrets.
In the United States:
The Chambers-Hiss affair,
The Robeson Peekskill riot,
The Greenglass-Rosenberg betrayal,
The trial of the top eleven REDS.
The RED trail in government offices;
These are the headlines
Of a thousand little scandals
In schools, colleges, churches,
Social agencies, trade unions,
Radio, movie, press, and theater.

4

RED STRATEGY

THE THIRTEEN MEN IN THE KREMLIN

Above the COMMUNIST PARTY
Sit the thirteen men of the Politburo,

This is the RED hierarchy
That controls all life in Russia,
That pulls the puppet wires of satellite states,
That directs the World strategy
To bring all people,   •
Under the yoke of the Kremlin.
This is the self-appointed
SUPER STATE
Of the Red Revolution
That Marx dreamed of,
That Lenin organized,
That Stalin rules.

HOW DO THEY WORK?

Tyrants mislead the people
By making them hate someone,
By blaming somebody for bad times.

27

The Roman emperors kept their people in hand
By blaming the Christians
And throwing them to the lions,
Or burning them at the stake.

In the Dark Ages
Political despots and misguided zealots

Turned on the Jews
To blame them for economic and political trouble.

In more recent times
The Catholics persecuted the Protestants
And the Protestants abused the Catholics
Because the unscrupulous leaders
Had to find somebody to blame for their woes.

Hitler revived this worn-out hate
Blaming the Jews for all the German woes.
He built up the Brown Shirt Storm Troopers
To "protect" gullible Germans from the Jews,
And then turned his S.S. rowdies
On all who dared oppose his Nazi gang;
Jews, Christians; Catholics, Protestants,
Laborers, executives, conservatives, liberals—
Called them enemies of the German people.

Now STALIN claims to protect the workers
From the middle classes
And leaders of the western nations;—
Imperialistic warmongers, decadent capitalists,

Corrupt middle class, exploiters of the poor,
Race discriminators, enemies of the common people.
These are the names the REDS use
To tag the new victims of persecution.
The new scapegoats!

STORM WARNINGS!

The record of 2000 years of history
Shows a clear storm warning.
When human rights are in danger,
Persecution of one group—a minority,
Is the danger signal.

For when one group is attacked
Persecution soon will spread to all
Who stand in the tyrant's way.

I. DIVISION—
    The Politburo has improved its tactics.
They claim to be the saviors
          of the oppressed
           the exploited
           the wronged
           the poor.

To divide their opposition they attack:
    Management to win labor,
    Storekeepers to win customers,

Industry to win farmers,
  Catholics to win Protestants,
    Conservatives to win liberals,
      Whites to win Negroes,
        The "Haves" to win the "Have Nots."
Thus does the RED hierarchy
Accent division among friendly people,
Magnifying classes
To build a classless society!

II. CONFUSION—

From the soil of confusion spring
The weeds of discontent and despair.
So no constructive action
Must be allowed to settle problems—
Economic, social, political, or cultural.

Every flicker of complaint
Must be fanned into the wild flames
Of rebellion.

Every positive program
Must be opposed;

Every disturbing condition
Must be aggravated.

People must feel
The hopelessness confusion!
Then they are open
To RED dogma
Of the false Utopia!

III. SABOTAGE—

It's SABOTAGE that gets results.
The word "sabotage" referred to sabots
Or wooden shoes worn by peasants
Who were clumsy, ignorant, wasteful.
So the word came to mean bungling waste,
And later clever bungling to destroy.

Today SABOTAGE takes in what we call
"Dropping a monkey wrench in the machinery":
High wastage in the shop, damaged machines,
Slanted news reports, missent letters,
Biased teaching, misrepresenting diplomacy.

33

Thousands and millions
Of these tiny unseen mistakes
Keep nibbling away at efficiency and production
Slowly destroying industry and commerce,
And weakening a nation for the RED kill.

IV. DESTRUCTION—

But the final RED weapon is destruction,
With the Four Horsemen running wild.

Karl Marx predicted that the day would come
When workers would rise up against their masters
In bloody revolution.

Lenin, Trotsky, Stalin
Predicted this final "class struggle"
When capitalism would be blotted out;
For they believe that
COMMUNISM can never exist safely
Until all its enemies are destroyed
And the Politburo rules the world.

Then will the workers live in peace and plenty.
From the blood of the non-Communists
Will rise the NEW RED WORLD
Of which they sing in their "Internationale,"
And for which they continually plan and work.

5

RUSSIAN MODEL FOR
THE NEW RED WORLD

THE PEOPLE—

200,000,000 live
In the Union of Soviet Socialist Republics.
From Baltic Sea to Pacific Ocean
From Arctic tundras to Ukrainian wheat fields,
Men, women, boys, girls,
Young, old, big, little,
Greedy, generous,
Hateful, friendly,
Wise, simple,
Good, bad,
All kinds that make a nation.

Eating, sleeping, working,
Planning, sharing, hoping,
Loving, mating, rearing their families,
Like all other people of the world,
But carrying the COMMUNIST system
On their backs.

THE PARTY—

6,000,000 members of the Communist Party.
THE ONLY PARTY.
These Party members are the Privileged Class
In classless Russia.

Members are admitted after long probation
In which they have proved their loyalty

their devotion

their zeal

For the Communist Cause.

Above the Party members rank the officers,
And the higher officers,
Up through the hierarchy
To the peak of authority
THE POLITBURO.

All recognition, reward, honor, glory
Is based on service
Not to the nation,

but to THE PARTY!

40

THE GOVERNMENT—

A "SOVIET" is an organized group of workers
In an industry or trade,
So people of a town or city
Are always divided between SOVIETS.

Small SOVIETS make up larger SOVIETS
All together making up
The Union of Soviet Socialist Republics.

The job of the SOVIETS
Is not to make laws,
But to act as a
                           Transmission belt
To carry out regulations.

Ruling government officials
Are chosen by the "wise" leaders
Of the COMMUNIST Party
And "elected" by the people's vote
For that one slate.

In Communist countries
People are not considered smart enough
To pick their leaders,
Just to vote for those the "wise ones" pick.

So the legal forms of government
From constitution down to town officials
Are maintained
To make the people think they rule,
But representatives and officeholders
Large and small
Are chosen from the PARTY
              by the PARTY
                for the PARTY.
For Russia is Communist
Not by choice of the people
But by the will of the

COMMUNIST PARTY.

FOOD, SHELTER, CLOTHING—

   How do the people get these necessities of life?
The posters and slogans

Say, "*Stalin will provide*,"
But millions of Russians know
They must shift for themselves
If they want to exist.
In the early years they took from the nobles
                                                the wealthy
                                                    the church
To provide for the "good" COMMUNISTS
But that supply soon ran short.
As it always must
Since what looks like the great wealth of the rich
Cannot amount to much
When divided among the many.

    Now these things must come from the people,
So the government takes from some
By quotas, allotments, and collections,
And gives to the faithful PARTY supporters.
By speech and press and radio
STALIN tells the Russian people
They will have food
                        housing
                            clothing
                                luxuries

43

Far surpassing the miserable people
Of capitalist-exploited countries;
But the stores don't get the supplies,
And what luxuries there are
Go to the COMMUNIST officials.
So the beautiful Communist slogan,
"To each according to his need"
Remains just that,

a slogan,

not a fact.

INDUSTRIES–

All industry in RUSSIA is government owned

government operated.

Government bureaus control all raw materials.
Great bureaus appointed by the POLITBURO
Decide—what shall be made

when it shall be made

where it shall be made

who shall make it

who shall get it.

Workers are allotted to industries
By government bureaus.
Men have no choice—what they will do

where they will work

They must work where they are assigned
Or suffer punishment
Or become fugitives from home
                    from friends
                        from government.

Training for good jobs
Goes to the PARTY faithful;
Advancement is only
For those who are ardent PARTY members;
Achievement comes only to those
Who stay in the good graces of PARTY leaders.
PARTY faithfulness is more important

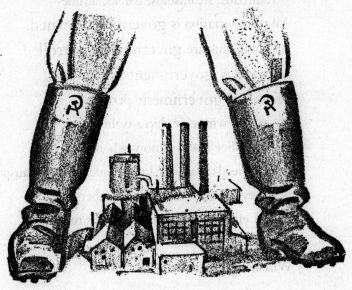

Than mere ability.
Failure to produce results
Can usually be blamed on assistants

                              unfaithful

                                    scapegoats,

Who can be punished
For the bureaucrat's mistakes.
This is Red Russia's blueprint for industry.

TRANSPORTATION–

   Railroads, steamships, trucks, airlines–
All transportation is government owned.
All shipments are government controlled.
All travel is government regulated.
People get government permits
To go anywhere or ship anything.
So the police always know where they are.
Bureau heads may not know much about transportation
But they are good PARTY members,
And if efficiency falls off, or trains run late,
Prison or executions
Will always improve performance.

46

It's all very simple when transportation
Is run for the convenience
                    of the government
Not for the service
                of the people.

FARMS—

   Food comes from farms
So farms must be controlled.
Peasants were forced into co-operatives
Where planting
                cultivating
                    harvesting
Can be done "under supervision"
Government bureaus decide what to plant
And the government collects all produce
So the farmers, like city workers,
Have to live—if they can—on rations.

When the Kulaks—independent farmers—
Refused to unite in co-operatives

Their food supply was cut off
And ten million men, women, and children starved
Or were shipped to Siberia as slave labor
As enemies of the State.
Because they tried to cling to some independence.

48

EDUCATION—

All children belong to the State
In Soviet Russia,
Not to their parents—who are unimportant—
So from the nursery to the university
The COMMUNIST government decides—
What shall be taught
Who shall teach it
How it shall be taught
To whom it shall be taught.

The rule is—
Education is the reward for PARTY loyalty.

COMMUNISM is taught like a religion
To young and old.
History, literature, science, art
Are strange subjects
Telling only the RED line.

All research and teaching must follow
The PARTY line.
Study is not to learn facts
But to learn what
The "great minds" of COMMUNISM have decided.
Research in science

        technology

          humanities

            art

Must not seek new and unknown facts
But must devise data that supports
The predetermined COMMUNIST theories.

This alone spells the doom of COMMUNISM
For this is the rule of suppression
That brought the Dark Ages
Not the goal of the enlightenment
That brought modern progress

            and civilization.

INFORMATION—

COMMUNISTS say they believe in

Freedom of the press—

Not freedom of the individual

To learn or tell the facts

But freedom of the government

To print what the people should be told

Without interference of the people

Without reference to the truth.

RED reporters do not rush to get the facts;
They wait to see what the "free" government
Decides shall be told the people.

So all information in Russia
Must conform to the PARTY line.
Laid down by the government.
Failure to follow this means death
imprisonment
Siberia for re-education.

ENTERTAINMENT and AMUSEMENT—

Music, Drama, Literature, Art—
These are the tools for implanting
The approved Communist ideas
In the minds of the people.

These are activities of the State.
Concerts, operas, plays, and circuses
Must spread the Communist line.
Artists, actors, writers, and musicians
Are showered with honors, and privileges,
As long as they follow the PARTY line.

So art is never a way
To express individual ideas,

52

Or great human inspirations;
But always—a tool of government
To put over the PARTY line—
"The scientific theory of dialectical materialism"
As outlined by the great authority—STALIN.

RELIGION—

It was KARL MARX who said:

"Religion is the opiate
by which the people
are kept in subjection."

53

NICOLAI LENIN preached this doctrine
And suppressed the church.
JOSEPH STALIN, who renounced the priesthood,
Hates religion as only the renegade can.

   So these "saints" of COMMUNISM
Have always fought against religion;
They have ridiculed those who clung to faith;
And taught youth—
That religion is stupid,

                    superstitious

                          opposed to COMMUNIST belief.

   They took over churches,

                cathedrals

                    institutions
For government uses as clubs or recreation halls.
Where they could not stamp out religion
They put the clergy under government control
To smother it in red tape.
   To take the place of the deep human urge
To reach out to a Divine Providence

54

That gives meaning to life
They have trumped up
A frenzied hero-worship

Of MARX,

of LENIN,

of STALIN

The "saints" of the new Red World.

WHAT MAKES THIS RED WORLD TICK?

FEAR—is the driving power
In the Communist world.

For STALIN—who came to power
By assassination of friend and foe—
It's fear some trusted aid will turn traitor.
He rules his staff—

> with terror.

For COMMUNIST PARTY OFFICERS
It's fear of the man above
> and the man below;
That one mistake,
> one failure
To follow THE PARTY LINE,
Or to fail to be in the right clique,
Will mean death or Siberia.

For COMMUNIST PARTY MEMBERS
It's fear
That they will not praise STALIN loudly enough;
That they will talk at the wrong time,

Or be silent when they should talk,
That they will associate with the wrong members
Or serve the wrong officers.

FOR THE PROBATIONER, young or old,
It's fear
That he will fail to become a PARTY member,
Through—lack of zeal
     failure to learn the line
       displeasing the right officers,
And thus be forever shut out
From the chosen few.

For all COMMUNISTS
It's fear
Of never being yourself,
Of never being sure you're right or wrong.
It's FEAR that makes the Red World tick.

SECRET POLICE

 Fear's strong arm
      is the Secret Police.

Because he was a revolutionary
LENIN developed the Secret Police.
They murdered the Czar and his family,
Nobles, merchants, manufacturers,
Scientists, teachers, doctors, lawyers.
This reign of terror established
The SECRET POLICE
As an institution in RED RUSSIA
With power of life and death.

STALIN who established his power
By purges of millions
Enlarged the SECRET POLICE.

This dread organization, M.V.D.

Has power of arrest

        trial

           sentence

              execution

Without courts of justice or defense.

Court trials are only shows for propaganda

With those who will confess their crimes,

Real or imaginary
Playing the grim roles.
Nobody knows who these Police may be,
Driven by FEAR—
  It's brother against brother,
        child against parent,
          student against teacher,
            worker against foreman,
              member against officer,
All in desperate terror
To save themselves
At any cost.

This secret FEAR—
The fear of spies, informers,
The fear of the dread
                    knock on the door
That means arrest—
That freezes men's hearts,
Compels abject obedience,
With threat of death and forced labor.

The example of
The 12 million miserable souls
In slave labor camps
Year after year,
Beside the millions executed
Year after year,
Provides the whip lash
Of the FEAR.

CIVILIZATION vs BARBARISM

Christian civilization
Built on the great principle
Of Jesus, the Master teacher,
"Love the Lord Thy God!"
and
"Love thy neighbor!"

But Marx, Lenin, and Stalin
Would take the world
Back to barbarism with
"Deny God" and
"Fear thy neighbor."

6

THE TROJAN HORSE AT WORK

THE RED PLAN OF ATTACK ON THE U.S.A.

If the strategy of the Politburo
Were put in the form of a directive
It would look something like this:

TOP SECRET

From: Politburo, The Kremlin, Moscow

To: Headquarters, Communist Party, U.S.A.

Subject: Preparation to Seize the U.S.A.

USE STANDARD OPERATING PROCEDURE PREPARING THE
UNITED STATES FOR SEIZURE BY COMMUNIST FORCES.
(1) INFILTRATE PRESS, RADIO, THEATER, MOVIES,
TELEVISION, LECTURE PLATFORM, AND ALL OTHER
INFORMATION SERVICES TO SPREAD COMMUNIST LINE;
(2) GET CONTROL OF LABOR UNIONS, AGITATE CON-
TINUAL LABOR TROUBLE; (3) GET MEMBERS AND
FELLOW-TRAVELERS INTO EDUCATIONAL AND SCIENTIFIC
ORGANIZATIONS; (4) TAKE OVER LIBERAL RELIGIOUS,
SOCIAL, AND POLITICAL REFORM MOVEMENTS;
(5) CAMPAIGN LOUDLY AGAINST WALL STREET,
IMPERIALISTS, WARMONGERS, AND MONOPOLY CAPITALISTS;
(6) KEEP KEY MEN IN GOVERNMENT AND INDUSTRY TO
REPORT SECRET POLICY DIRECTIVES, AND CREATE NATIONAL
CONFUSION AND INTERNATIONAL FRICTION.

(*signed*) JOSEPH STALIN

THE APPARATUS

The COMMUNIST underground apparatus
Is the CELL—
A group of secret operatives
Bound together as a working unit
To do an assigned job.
Members of the cell may not know each other;
They take orders from the leader;
Report to him their actions.
They must stay secret
To do their undercover work.
Fear of failure and punishment
Or betrayal as spies and traitors
Is the force that drives them on
To take step after step—
Red Footprints of the Trojan Horse.

FOOTPRINT—

(1) "INFILTRATE PRESS, RADIO, MOVIES, THEATER,
TELEVISION, LECTURE PLATFORM, AND ALL
OTHER INFORMATION SERVICES TO SPREAD THE
COMMUNIST LINE."

The first step
Is to poison the springs of truth.

67

Working for newspapers, magazines, radio,
Movies, T.V., theater, lecture platform,
These members of COMMUNIST cells
Spread criticism and indirect attacks
On American customs, and institutions
Arousing resentment and rebellious attitudes,
Ridiculing the virtues of good citizens,
Scoffing at the motives of trusted leaders.
Seeds of rebellion are sown quietly
So that good people never know
That they are being softened up
For propaganda.

   Then come the rosy pictures
Of the new world, classless society,
                    rule by the workers
                      freed from the exploiter;
Pictures of "brotherhood of all races,"
Good things for all laborers,
That the cruel capitalists
Have kept from them;
Demands for civil rights
Freedom from discrimination.
Such footprints of the Trojan Horse
Pollute the springs of truth.

FOOTPRINT—

(2) "GET CONTROL OF LABOR UNIONS;

AGITATE CONTINUAL LABOR TROUBLE."

*Lenin wrote: "For revolution it is essential that
a majority of workers should fully understand that
revolution is necessary and be ready to sacrifice
their lives for it."* *

*Again: "Revolution is impossible without nation-wide
crisis."* *

There is the program.
Labor must be used to fight the battle
And to create conditions for revolution.
First — Get key men in top union jobs
By winning over present officers
Or by getting cell members elected.

How far this plan is on its way
Is proved by the fight patriotic leaders

* Lenin, *Selected Works*, Vol. X, p. 127.

69

Are waging to drive REDS out of—

Electrical workers,

Dock workers,

Auto workers,

Farm implement workers,

Mine and smelter workers,

and many others

Second —The ever-recurring strikes

stoppages

sick leaves

That cut down operation
Of industries, stores, transportation,
Increasing costs, spreading confusion,
Led too often by over-zealous officers
Unconsciously following the COMMUNIST line.
These are footprints of the Trojan Horse
Showing plainly the tracks to RED REVOLUTION.

FOOTPRINT—

(3) "GET MEMBERS AND FELLOW-TRAVELERS INTO
EDUCATIONAL AND SCIENTIFIC ORGANIZATIONS."

It is not enough to spread COMMUNIST ideas
Among grown-ups
They must be taught to children and youth
Who will carry the RED banners.

So COMMUNISTS drive to win followers
Among the teachers,
school administrators,
university professors
Who guide the education of young people.

And even more important
Is the infiltration of the student groups.
Only a continual fight
Has saved the National Student Association
From being taken by the REDS.

Then, too, the best developments
Of science and technology
Coming out of the university laboratory
Must be picked up
And passed on to the SOVIET.
So the Politburo must have its Fuchs

and Rosenbergs.
Thus the Red Trojan Horse moves in
To capture education and pure science.

FOOTPRINT—

(4) "TAKE OVER LIBERAL RELIGIOUS, SOCIAL,
AND POLITICAL REFORM MOVEMENTS."

The greatest progress for human betterment
Has come in the United States

Where religious and social leaders
Are free to point out wrongs
And press for greater equality

> justice

> > opportunity

And when humane leaders
Have shown the need
And proved ways to meet those needs
Then great business leaders
Have provided funds to launch
New movements and reforms;
And political leaders
Have provided legal aids
To bring new human progress.

Thus religion, government, and business—
Yes, the very capitalism REDS condemn—
Have teamed up to give Americans
Hospitals, schools, better living,
Social welfare, beyond compare.

But COMMUNISTS dare not let the people
Know this fact.
They must claim the credit,
And so they seek to steal the leadership

In these progressive movements,
By infiltration — footprints of the Trojan Horse.

FOOTPRINT—

(5) "CAMPAIGN LOUDLY AGAINST WALL STREET, IM-
PERIALISTS, WARMONGERS, MONOPOLY CAPITAL-
ISTS."

*Says Stalin: "Under capitalism, the exploited masses do
not, nor can they really participate in the administration
of the country, if for no other reason, than that under
conditions of capitalism, governments are not set up by
the people, but by the Rockefellers and Morgans . . .
Capitalist democracy is democracy of the exploiting
minority based on the restriction of the rights of the
exploited majority."* *

Wall Street, imperialists, warmongers,
Monopoly capitalists, corrupt politicians—
These must be blamed for troubles,
Real or imaginary, in the U.S.A.;

* Stalin, *Problems of Leninism*, pp. 43 & 44.

74

The workers must be made to hate
The men they are to rebel against.

And furthermore there must be loud clamor
To draw attention away from the devious ways
Of the RED underground
Lining the workers against
Their future enemies.
Such noisy clamor aims
To distract the unwary
And draw the crowds.

75

FOOTPRINT—

(6) "KEEP KEY MEN IN GOVERNMENT AND INDUSTRY
    TO REPORT SECRET POLICY DIRECTIVES AND CREATE
    NATIONAL CONFUSION AND INTERNATIONAL FRIC-
    TION!"

MARX, LENIN, STALIN have agreed
That Communism could never win
Against "capitalist nations"

                    Unless they were divided;
Fighting each other
In wars for "spheres of influence"
            "raw materials"
            "markets"
and "colonial rebellions."

    To foment these the POLITBURO
Must have secret information,
Inside men in government and industry
To agitate conflict
Among "capitalist" people,
That will wear down their strength
And weaken them for COMMUNIST inroads.

76

How much of the trouble in
   Greece and Israel
      Germany and Austria
         China and Korea
            India and Iran
               and other trouble spots
Is built up by this tactic
Of the Red Trojan Horse?

FOOTPRINTS MAKE A TRACK

These six important footprints
And many lesser ones
Are steps that beat a track
Whose trail leads from Moscow
Throughout all the world,
Even to America.

Troy fought the Greeks
For ten long years
Fought valiantly with arms,
But fell
A victim to that Trojan Horse.

Americans!

What of the Red Footprints
Of the Trojan Horse?

7

AMERICA'S DEFENSE

Four centuries
Have brought millions of people
To America,
Fleeing from oppression
             regulation
               exploitation
To find a home
Where they could live their own lives.
Where there is freedom
           justice
             equality
               opportunity
Where there are no rulers
But all rule.
Here they built a NEW WORLD!

Twice in a generation
The United States has had to help defeat
Ruthless aggressors bent on world conquest—
Kaiser Wilhelm, Hitler, Mussolini, Tojo—
Who believed in the power of military might

> *But forgot the power of ideas.*

Now Stalin makes a new bid for conquest
By Communist ideas

> *Backed up by military might.*

Already he has swept millions under his power
And is slowly drawing other millions.
What is the answer to this strategy?

AMERICA'S ANSWER!

In man's rise from barbarism,
We've slowly learned
That the answer to a club

> *is a better club;*

the answer to a gun

> *is a better gun;*

the answer to a warship

> *is a better warship;*

the answer to an airplane

> *is a better airplane;*

So we know that the answer to an idea

> *is a better idea.*

And the answer to the idea of COMMUNISM

Backed up by the RED ARMY
Is a better idea—the American idea—
Backed up, if necessary,
By the AMERICAN defense forces
That never lost a war!

THE AMERICAN IDEA!

We believe:
That it starts with the individual
                    the person
                              the human soul
Worth more than all else.
The world was made for MAN
Not man for the world.

Man is here to live
            to conquer his surroundings
            to create better things
            to be himself
                to be a good neighbor

"To be himself,
            at his best,
                    all the time!"

We believe:
THAT THE INDIVIDUAL MUST BE
FREE:

Free — to learn for himself
            to think for himself
            to act for himself

Free — to live where he will
            to come and go as he will
            to hold property as he will
            to work where he will
            and at what he will

Free — to associate with others
　　　　to pick his friends
　　　　　to worship as he chooses

We believe:
THAT THE INDIVIDUAL MUST BE
RESPONSIBLE:

Responsible—for what he thinks
　　　　　for what he says
　　　　　　for what he does

Responsible—for his property
　　　　　for his job
　　　　　　for his family

Responsible—for his share of government
　　　　　　for his community life
　　　　　　　for his church
　　　　　　　for his welfare

We believe:

THAT THERE MUST BE FREE
INSTITUTIONS TO SERVE
THE INDIVIDUAL

Freedom of Religion—

Many of the founding fathers
Came to America
So that they might worship God as they believed.

This is the foundation
Of man's faith in himself
And the world he lives in.

Freedom of Speech and Press—
  The only safe public policy
Is based on informed opinion.
For this there must be
Liberty to write and speak
So all can be informed.

Freedom of Assembly and Petition—
　　To create public opinion
Men must have the right
To convince or be convinced.
This means the right to assemble
Where discussion can take place.
And further, freedom can exist
Only if the people have the right
To petition government directly,
To protest wrongs.

Free Courts of Justice—
    To right wrongs
      To punish offenders
        To protect the oppressed
There must be courts of law
With fair and equal justice for all,
And security of person and property.

Free Competitive Enterprise—
    America has grown great
Because men have continually found

New things to grow;

        New ways of growing them;

New things to make;

        New ways of making them;

New things to do;

        New ways of doing them.

This struggle to do something better
Or quicker, or cheaper
Has given America the world's greatest progress
In meeting human need.
This freedom to do the job better

        And profit by it,

Is the foundation for prosperity
That brought the finer things of life.

We believe:
THAT INTELLIGENT AND WILLING CO-OPERATION BRINGS TRUE PROGRESS.

Impatient, overbearing men
Are always planning for other people
Telling them what to do,
Making them do it,
As if people cannot act for themselves.
Such progress never lasts.

True progress comes when people understand
What needs to be done
And do it willingly,
Co-operating with other like-minded people.
This kind of progress lasts.
This is the American Way.

THE AMERICAN IDEA

We act!
  The best beliefs
May be only idle dreams
Unless they are put to work!

  Our forefathers dreamed
And their dreams were the stuff
From which they forged their deeds.
Their dreams of a new world
Inspired them to cross the sea,
To build their homes and towns,
To push the frontier westward
In spite of untold hardship.

And all the while they built
The new life we call American,
With homes, schools, churches,
Farms, industries, commerce,
A great systemless system
That served men's needs
Because each sought to serve
And profit by that service.

And through it all developed government—
Town, county, state, and federal—
Preserving order, safeguarding justice,
Insuring freedom for each person
To live, to plan, to act
For his own best interests
And therefore for the good of all!
True self-government!

This life was built by active men
Who worked hard for themselves
But also took their part
In the common life of the neighborhood.
They built their schools

And churches
And organizations
To provide the better things
And promote new ideas.
Here in this voluntary association
To extend man's vision
And improve his living
They wove the very warp and woof
                    of self-government.

Today the Kremlin knows—
As Hitler did, and Mussolini too—
The way to control people
Is through their thoughts
            their associations
                their activities
So the first RED Target
Will always be the organizations
                    associations
                        societies
                            clubs
                                unions
Through which the people

94

Think, discuss, and act—
These tap roots of democracy
That must be kept strong and sound.

 It's not enough to do your job,
To earn your bread,
To care for your family,
Do this much and no more
And you invite RED victory.

       Alone you cannot win!

 A million million offices
In towns, counties, states, nation,
In schools and churches,
In clubs, associations, groups,
Must be filled wisely
With those who serve devotedly.
This is the mechanism
By which American ideals
Are translated into action.

 Every corrupt officeholder,
Every lazy committeeman

Is a blow against self-government.
Every time you say "I'm too busy"
Or "I'm not interested"
Or "I'm not wasting my time"
You aid the Kremlin's cause.

A thousand thousand "eager beavers,"
Members of Communist cells,
Or stupid fellow-travelers
Have already wormed their way
Into office and committee membership,
To poison or corrupt
Our organizations' programs and activities;
And even to take them over
As "fronts" for the Trojan Horse.

The only answer to this threat
Is the old one of the Minute Man—
Every loyal true AMERICAN
Ready to do his share
With his own resources
To fight with his neighbors
To defend this land.

When we put our beliefs
Into action
To make our AMERICAN ideals
Live as they should in our homes, schools, churches,
Towns, societies, associations,
The Kremlin will be helpless
For its mightiest weapon
Will be blunted, useless;
We will have overcome

the Trojan Horse

The enemy within,
With our own strength within!

TAKE YOUR CHOICE!

U.S.S.R.	U.S.A.
Lenin	Washington
One Party	Many Parties
Rule by One Class	Government by All
Secret Police—M.V.D.	Courts of Justice
State Monopolies	Competitive Enterprise
The Party Line	Free Public Opinion
Soviets	Local Government
Politburo	Elected Congress
Controlled Education	Free Schools
Freedom of the Party	Freedom of the Individual
Collective Farms	Independent Farmers
Huge Aggressive Army	Limited Defense Forces
Exploitation of Neighbors	Assistance to Neighbors
Propaganda Ministry	Free Information Agencies
Religious Repression	Freedom of Religion
Compulsion	Voluntary Co-operation
Stalin—the Dictator	Lincoln—The Emancipator
FEAR YOUR NEIGH-BOR	LOVE YOUR NEIGH-BOR

98

. . . "It is for us, the living, rather to be
dedicated . . . to the great unfinished work . . .
that this nation under God shall have a new birth
of freedom, and that government of the people, by
the people, and for the people shall not perish
from the earth."

GARY LIBRARY
VERMONT COLLEGE